Apollo
Fascinating Facts For
Kids

Rod Weston

This book is just one of a series of "Fascinating Facts For Kids" books. For more fascinating facts about people, history, animals, and much more please visit:

www.fascinatingfactsforkids.com

Contents

The Space Race

1.   Following the end of World War Two the United States and the Soviet Union were competing with each other for the control of space. The Americans were worried that if the Soviet Union could dominate space then they could dominate the world.

2.   The Soviets took the lead in the "Space Race" in October 1957, when they launched "Sputnik 1," the first ever man-made satellite, into orbit around the world. More success came in April 1962, when the Soviet cosmonaut, Yuri Gagarin, became the first human being to reach space and orbit the Earth.

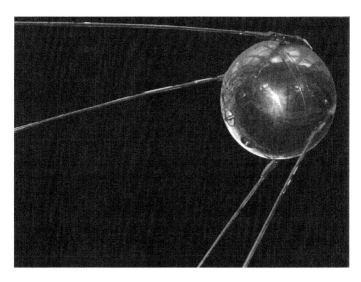

A replica of Sputnik 1

3. The United States had many early setbacks in the Space Race, but three weeks after Gagarin's historic flight, they responded by sending the first American, Alan Shepard, into space. His flight lasted just fifteen minutes and didn't reach Earth orbit, but it proved that America could at last compete with the Soviet Union.

Alan Shepard in space

4. The United States was now confident of beating the Soviet Union in the race to control space. In May 1961, President John F. Kennedy pledged that America would send a man to the Moon and bring him safely back to Earth before the end of the decade - just eight years away.

President John F. Kennedy

5.   President Kennedy promised the US space agency, NASA, all the money it needed for the challenging goal of landing a man on the Moon, and it set about making that dream come true.

Mercury & Gemini

6. Before attempting to land on the Moon, NASA needed to find out if human beings could survive for long periods in the harsh environment of space. The Mercury and Gemini programs would prove that it was possible.

The first Mercury astronauts

7. The third manned Mercury flight in February 1962, saw astronaut John Glenn become the first American to orbit the Earth. His five-hour mission saw him fly round the world three times before landing safely back on Earth.

John Glenn

8. The Gemini program followed Mercury, and each flight took two astronauts into orbit where they spent up to two weeks living in space. They carried out spacewalks to see if a man could survive outside his spacecraft while being kept alive by his spacesuit.

***Astronaut Ed White during his
spacewalk***

9.   As well as testing an astronaut's ability to
live and work for long periods in space, Gemini
was also used to practice and perfect the docking
of spacecraft. Docking is when two spacecraft
attach themselves to each other while traveling
through space at great speed - a procedure that
would be needed on a mission to the Moon.

10.   Mercury and Gemini were both great
successes and proved that it should be possible
to send a man to the Moon and return him safely
to Earth. The Gemini missions were followed by
the Apollo program, which would carry out even
more testing and preparation in order to send a
man on the long journey to the Moon.

The Apollo Spacecraft

11. Three spacecraft were needed for a mission to land men on the Moon. A massive, powerful rocket would blast off into orbit above the Earth. It would carry three astronauts and two other smaller spacecraft.

12. Attached to the top of the giant rocket would be the second spacecraft - the Command/Service Module. The third spacecraft - the Lunar Module - would be packed in tightly behind, and would be pulled free and docked with the Command/Service Module when in space. It would be the Lunar Module that would land two astronauts on the Moon.

Saturn V

13. It would need an incredibly fast and powerful rocket to enable a crew of three astronauts and all their equipment to escape Earth's gravity, so NASA engineers designed and built the biggest, heaviest, and most powerful rocket ever built - the Saturn V.

14. The Saturn V rocket stood 363 feet (111 m) tall - as high as a thirty-six-story building. It was three times taller than the Gemini rockets and four times taller than the rockets used in the Mercury program.

The Saturn V

15. The Saturn V was built in three sections - or "stages" - each filled with massive quantities of rocket fuel. When the first two stages had used up their fuel, they would separate from the rest of the rocket and fall back to Earth. The third stage would be used to propel the Command/ Service Module towards the Moon, after which it would separate before traveling deeper into space and going into orbit around the Sun.

The Command/Service Module

16. The cone-shaped Command Module was where the astronauts lived and worked during the trip to the Moon, and connected to it was the Service Module which supplied the Command Module with power, oxygen, and water.

The Command/Service Module

17. The Command Module was the nerve center of the journey to the Moon, and it contained the instruments and controls which enabled the astronauts to fly the spacecraft on the right course. It was the only part of the Saturn V which returned to Earth under control - all the other parts either fell back to Earth, remained in space, or were left on the Moon.

The Lunar Module

18. The Lunar Module was designed specifically for landing on the Moon. As there is no atmosphere on the Moon, the spacecraft didn't need to be streamlined or aerodynamic, and it looked unlike any other rocket ever built. Although it looked flimsy and fragile, it was a fine, robust spacecraft and was said to fly like a "nimble, responsive jet fighter."

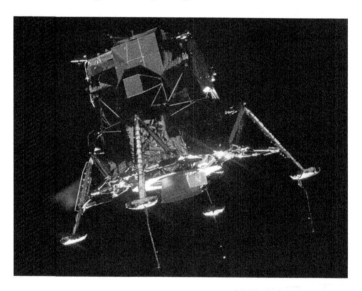

The Lunar Module

19. The Lunar Module was built in two sections. The lower "Descent Stage" included the four long legs which would touch down on the Moon's surface, the engines to control the descent, and the fuel tanks.

20. The top half of the Lunar Module - the "Ascent Stage" - contained the crew's cabin and all the instruments and controls. When the mission was over, the Ascent Stage would use its own engine to blast off from the Moon using the Descent Stage as a launch pad.

The Apollo Program

21. The Apollo program followed the successes of Mercury and Gemini, and each manned mission would see a crew of three astronauts being launched into space on board the Saturn V rocket. When the time came to land on the Moon, two of the astronauts would descend to the surface in the Lunar Module, while the third astronaut would remain in control of the Command Module in orbit around the Moon.

22. The first mission of the Apollo program was due for launch in February 1967, but tragedy struck a month earlier when the crew lost their lives during a pre-flight test which went wrong. A fire swept through the Command Module killing astronauts Virgil "Gus" Grissom, Ed White, and Roger Chaffee.

Gus Grissom, Ed White & Roger Chaffee

23. The Apollo 1 tragedy saw the Apollo program pause for nearly a year as lessons were learned and changes made, to ensure that nothing like it ever happened again. The Apollo 2 and Apollo 3 missions were canceled, and the program started again on November 9, 1967, with the launch of Apollo 4.

24. Between January 1968 and May 1969, there were six more Apollo missions. Each mission built on the previous one, testing and perfecting everything needed to pave the way for the mission which would finally see men walk on the Moon.

25. The Apollo 11 mission, which launched on July 16, 1969, achieved President Kennedy's goal when on July 21, Neil Armstrong and Buzz Aldrin became the first human beings to walk on the Moon. They returned to Earth safely two and a half days later.

Neil Armstrong   *Buzz Aldrin*

26. Four months after Apollo 11, a successful Apollo 12 mission saw two more men walk on the Moon's surface. Apollo 13, due for launch on April 11, 1970, would be the next mission to attempt the dangerous 240,000 mile (385,000 km) journey to the Moon.

The Crew & the Mission

27. The Mission Commander of Apollo 13 was forty-two-year-old Jim Lovell. He was a former test pilot in the US Navy and joined NASA in 1963. Lovell was the most experienced of NASA's astronauts, having flown in two Gemini missions and on Apollo 8, which was the first mission to orbit the Moon. He had spent nearly 600 hours in space.

Jim Lovell

28. The Command Module Pilot, thirty-eight-year-old Jack Swigert, had been a US Air Force pilot before joining NASA in 1966. He had been part of Apollo 13's backup crew, but three days before the launch he replaced Ken Mattingly in the main crew. Mattingly had been exposed to German measles and had no immunity to the disease. NASA didn't want to risk him falling ill during the mission, and so Swigert took his place.

Jack Swigert

29. Thirty-six-year-old Fred Haise was the Lunar Module Pilot for Apollo 13. He had joined NASA at the same time as Jack Swigert, and was also a former US Air Force pilot. Haise had been a member of the backup crews for Apollo 8 and Apollo 11.

Fred Haise

30. Gene Kranz was the Flight Director of Apollo 13, in charge of a team of engineers and Flight Directors at Mission Control in Houston. He had been Flight Director for Apollo 11, the mission that landed the first men on the Moon in July 1969. Kranz was responsible for the safety of the astronauts and the overall success of the mission.

Gene Kranz

31. Mission Control would be in constant radio contact with the crew of Apollo 13 during their journey to the Moon and back, and the Flight Controllers would monitor every component of the spacecraft to make sure it was functioning properly.

Mission Control

32. Unlike the previous two Apollo missions which landed on flat ground, Apollo 13 would attempt a more dangerous landing on a mountainous part of the Moon. The rock in the Moon's hills and mountains are older than in the flat areas, and scientists wanted samples of these older rocks brought back to Earth to be analyzed and studied.

Launch Day

33. The launch of Apollo 13 was scheduled for Saturday April 11, 1970, at 1:13 p.m. from NASA's launch complex at Cape Canaveral, Florida.

34. Lovell, Swigert, and Haise were woken from their sleep just before 9.00 a.m. and were given a final medical examination to make sure they were in top physical shape.

35. Three and a half hours before launch the astronauts sat down to a breakfast of steak, eggs, toast, orange juice, and coffee before being helped into their bulky spacesuits.

Haise & Lovell at breakfast

36. Having got into their spacesuits, the crew was driven to the launch pad where the Saturn V stood attached to the launch tower. An elevator took the three men to the top of the launch tower from where they could enter the spacecraft.

37. Lovell, Swigert, and Haise took their seats in the Command Module two hours and forty minutes before launch time. They carried out checks and procedures to make sure every part of the spacecraft was in order and ready for liftoff.

38. Shortly before 1:13 p.m. the final countdown began and the Saturn V engines burst into life. When they were at full power the rocket was released from the launch tower, and it rose into the air on a massive column of smoke and flames.

The launch of Apollo 13

39.   The Saturn V accelerated to a tremendous speed - after just two and a half minutes it was moving at more than 6,000 miles per hour (9,650 kph), pushing the astronauts back into their seats and making them feel four times heavier than normal.

40.   The rocket had been lifted into the air by the first stage and when its fuel was used up, at an altitude of around forty-two miles (68 km), it was discarded and fell back to Earth. Stage two then took over.

41.   Five minutes into the mission one of stage two's five engines cut out two minutes earlier than it should have. Engineers at Mission Control in Houston decided that the remaining four engines had enough power to keep the spacecraft flying, and sent a radio message to the astronauts saying that they wouldn't have to abort the mission.

42.   The Flight Director at Mission Control, Gene Kranz, knew that every mission was likely to have a glitch, or a moment when a piece of equipment malfunctions. He was relieved that Apollo 13's was over and done with so early.

43.   Once stage two had done its job, the third stage burned for two minutes, sending Apollo 13 into orbit just thirteen minutes after liftoff. When the engine was shut down, the spacecraft continued traveling 115 miles (185 km) above

Earth at a speed of 17,500 miles per hour (28,000 kph).

44. The three astronauts carried out checks to make sure the spacecraft was ready to break free of Earth's gravity and head for the Moon. When the checks were done the engine of the third stage was fired again. It burned for more than six minutes, providing "Trans-Lunar Injection," which increased the speed to 24,000 miles per hour (38,600 kph), pushing the spacecraft out of Earth's orbit.

Earth seen from Apollo 13

45. At around three hours into the mission the third stage was released and the Command/Service Module was traveling under its own power. The third stage still contained the Lunar Module which needed to be attached to the Command Module.

46. Four panels had opened in the third stage where the Lunar Module was stored. Swigert, the Command Module Pilot, turned his spaceship around and headed to the Lunar Module where he could dock the two spacecraft. With the Lunar Module securely attached to the front of the Command Module, Swigert turned around again and gave his engine a two-second burst which sent Apollo 13 on its journey to the Moon.

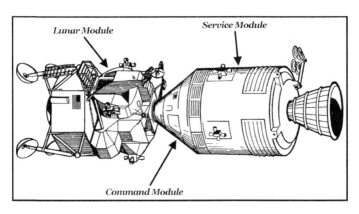

To the Moon

47. The journey to the Moon would be spent resting, eating, and making sure the spacecraft stayed in good working order. The crew had been able to take off their heavy spacesuits and wore much more comfortable two-piece nylon jumpsuits.

48. Enough food and water for the ten-day mission had been packed on board the spaceship. NASA scientists had developed a nutritionally balanced menu of dehydrated and freeze-dried food, and the astronauts were able to enjoy meals such as beef stew and chicken soup.

49. On day three of the mission the crew sent TV pictures back to Earth so people could see how they lived and worked in space. Unlike on previous missions to the Moon, however, hardly anyone was watching. After two successful trips to the Moon, most Americans had lost interest in the Apollo program - it had become too predictable and routine.

50. Apollo 13's journey had been uneventful so far. The only problems had been the engine failure after launch and erratic readings from one of the oxygen tanks in the Service Module. It looked like the mission was going to be a great success.

Explosion

51. Apollo 13's supply of oxygen was stored in two tanks in the Service Module. The temperature inside the tanks was so low that the oxygen turned into a frozen slush. Every now and then, the slush had to be stirred to warm it up a little.

52. Around fifty-six hours into the journey, Mission Control in Houston asked the Apollo crew to turn on fans to stir the oxygen tanks. Jack Swigert flipped a switch and moments later there was a loud bang. The lights went out in the Command Module and dozens of alarms started beeping and flashing. Swigert radioed to Mission Control, "Houston, we've had a problem here."

53. Jim Lovell looked out of the Command Module's window and saw gas escaping into space. Afraid it might be oxygen, he went to the control panel to check the oxygen tanks. One tank was completely empty and the other was emptying fast.

54. At Mission Control, Gene Kranz knew that one of the oxygen tanks must have exploded and damaged the Command Module's power supply. Without oxygen to breathe and power to keep the spaceship functioning, the astronauts were in serious trouble 200,000 miles (320,000 km) from Earth.

55. Every minute the astronauts spent in the Command Module the more of its power they used. If they were to get back to Earth, the Command Module would be needed for the re-entry through the atmosphere, and without power the spaceship would be useless.

56. The journey through Earth's atmosphere during re-entry reaches a speed of 20,000 miles per hour (32,000 kph) and the friction generated produces a temperature of around 5,000°F (2,760°C). The Command Module was the only part of Apollo 13 with a heat shield to prevent the spacecraft from burning up.

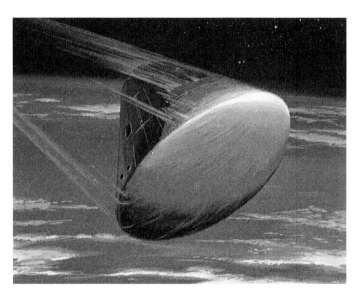

The heat shield at re-entry

57. The Lunar Module, which was attached to the front of the Command Module, had its own separate oxygen and power supplies, so Kranz told the Apollo crew to shut down all remaining power in the Command Module and move into the Lunar Module. The engineers and scientists at Mission Control could then try and come up with a plan to get Apollo 13 back to Earth.

The Plan

58. The quickest way to get home would be to turn the spacecraft around and use the Service Module's engine to send Apollo on its way back to Earth. Getting home this way would take around thirty-four hours, and the Lunar Module would have enough power to complete the journey.

59. But Gene Kranz was not keen on using the Service Module's engine. He was worried that it might have been damaged in the explosion and that it could blow up the whole spaceship, killing the crew instantly.

60. The second way to get back to Earth was to use a "free-return." Apollo would continue on its journey and fly into orbit round the Moon. Lunar gravity would speed up the spacecraft and sling it back towards Earth.

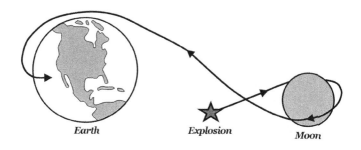

Earth   Explosion   Moon

The "free-return"

61. The free-return method would take longer than simply turning round. It would be four days before Apollo reached Earth and the Lunar Module would run out of power in less than seventy hours. But Kranz had decided that the free-return would be safer and he told his engineers at Mission Control to find ways of saving the Lunar Module's power.

Behind the Moon

62. As Apollo continued on its journey to the Moon, Mission Control got the astronauts to turn off the power to anything that wasn't essential. Lights and heating were switched off, and the spacecraft became dark and bitterly cold.

63. With the temperature at just above freezing, the whole spacecraft became wet as moisture from the astronauts' breath condensed on the walls, instrument panels, and windows. Drinking water was also a problem with only enough for each astronaut to have less than one glass a day. It was going to be an uncomfortable journey home.

64. As the spaceship got closer to the Moon, it was pulled into orbit by lunar gravity. Radio contact was lost as it flew behind the Moon, but when communication was possible again, Mission Control got the crew to fire up the Lunar Module's engine for four minutes. This would propel the spaceship out of lunar orbit and increase speed so that Apollo could get back to Earth before all power was lost.

The Journey Home

65. The Lunar Module was fitted with special filters that trapped the carbon dioxide exhaled out by its two-man crew. But with three men breathing out the poisonous gas, the filter would soon become full and be unable to hold any more. Mission Control calculated that the astronauts would die from carbon dioxide poisoning two days before they reached Earth.

66. The Command Module also had carbon dioxide filters but they were square in shape, and the Lunar Module's were round. A way had to be found of fitting a square filter into the Lunar Module.

67. Using the exact same materials that the astronauts had on the Apollo spacecraft, a team of engineers at Mission Control got to work to find a way of making a new filter. Using materials including cardboard, a roll of tape, hoses, and a plastic bag, they managed to make a workable filter which they told the astronauts how to build.

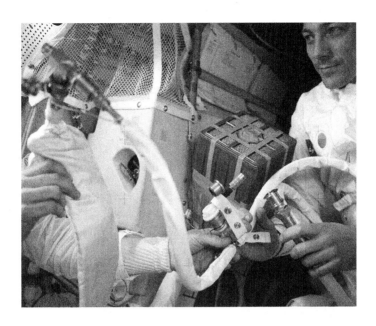

Jack Swigert with the new filter

68. As the carbon dioxide levels in the Lunar Module got dangerously high, the astronauts spent an hour building the new filter. When they fitted it, the filter began to do its job, meaning the Apollo crew could get back to Earth alive.

Re-Entry and Splashdown

69. By the morning of April 17, Apollo 13 was just hours away from Earth and the crew needed to prepare for re-entry. They would have to move back into the Command Module and turn on what power it had left to make the dangerous trip through Earth's atmosphere.

70. When the astronauts entered the freezing-cold Command Module, their breath and the heat from their bodies saw condensation form on the windows and instrument panel. They were worried that the water would destroy the electrical connections when the power was switched on. But all they could do was hope.

71. Four hours before re-entry, Jack Swigert flipped a switch to release the Service Module from the Command Module. As they looked out of the window the crew could see that the explosion had blown a whole side of the spacecraft away, leaving a big hole with dangling wires and pieces of metal.

The damaged Service Module

72. Two and a half hours from re-entry, the crew began powering up the Command Module. Thirty minutes later, when the spacecraft was up and running, a switch was flipped which released the Lunar Module from the Command Module. When the Lunar Module had floated off into space the astronauts strapped themselves into their seats to begin re-entry.

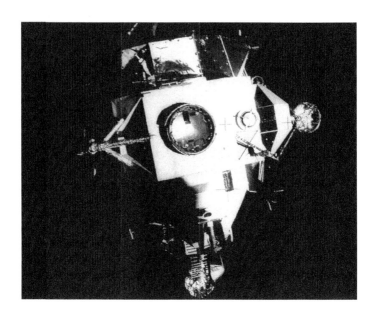

The Lunar Module floats off into space

73. Re-entry is dangerous even in a fully-working spacecraft, but it would be even more risky for Apollo 13. The heat shield might have been damaged in the explosion, the wet instrument panel could stop working, or the Command Module could run out of power. There was no way of knowing if the crew would survive.

74. As the Command Module descended through the atmosphere at 20,000 miles per hour (32,000 kph) the heat generated blocked out all radio signals. Nobody at Mission Control or the millions watching on TV knew if the astronauts were alive or dead.

75. After three minutes of radio silence Mission Control tried calling Apollo 13, but there was no answer. After four long minutes the voice of Jack Swigert finally came over the radio. Apollo 13's parachutes had successfully opened and the Command Module was about to land safely in the Pacific Ocean.

Splashdown in the Pacific

Successful Failure

76. NASA was able to find out how an electrical fault had caused the explosion that destroyed Apollo 13's Service Module. They fixed the problem and would send four more successful missions the Moon.

77. Gene Kranz was very proud of how his team at Mission Control had performed, and he was awarded the Presidential Medal of Freedom Team Award. He remained an important person at NASA until his retirement in 1994.

78. Apollo 13 was Jim Lovell's last flight into space, and he retired as an astronaut in 1973. He went on to write a book about the Apollo 13 mission which was made into a movie starring Tom Hanks as the Mission Commander.

79. Apollo 13 was Jack Swigert's only space flight and he retired from NASA in 1973. He ran for Congress in 1982, but died before he could take office.

80. Fred Haise became a member of the Apollo 16 backup crew and would probably have gone to the Moon again if the Apollo program hadn't been canceled in 1972. He worked on NASA's Space Shuttle program before retiring in 1979.

81. Ken Mattingly never did get German measles and got his chance to go to the Moon in 1972 as Commander of Apollo 16.

Commander Ken Mattingly

82. Although Apollo 13 didn't land a man on the Moon, it became known as a "successful failure." The astronauts failed to walk on the Moon, but they and the team at Mission Control succeeded in pulling off one of the most remarkable rescues ever attempted.

Illustration Attributions

A replica of Sputnik 1
NSSDC, NASA

Cover & final image (Apollo 13 insignia) : Alan Shepard in space : President John F. Kennedy : The first Mercury astronauts : John Glenn : Astronaut Ed White during his spacewalk : The Saturn V : The Command/Service Module : The Lunar Module : Neil Armstrong : Buzz Aldrin : Jack Swigert : Fred Haise : Mission Control : Haise and Lovell at breakfast : The launch of Apollo 13 : Earth seen from Apollo 13 : The Lunar Module attached to the Command Module : The heat shield at re-entry : The "free-return" :
The Lunar Module floats off into space :
Splashdown in the Pacific
NASA [Public domain]

Gus Grissom, Ed White & Roger Chaffee
NASA / Photographer unknown

Jim Lovell
NASA photographer [Public domain]

Gene Kranz
NASA; Restored by Adam Cuerden [Public domain]

Jack Swigert with the new filter
Kim Dismukes [Public domain]

The damaged Service Module
NASAScan by Kipp Teague [Public domain]

Commander Ken Mattingly
Unknown author NASA [Public domain]

Printed in Great Britain
by Amazon